Jade Summ[er]

MW00475204

COLORING BOOKS FOR EVERYONE

Thank you for purchasing our coloring book!

We hope you have a fun and relaxing experience when coloring.

Everyone who worked on this book appreciates your support.

Fritzen Publishing LLC is a Delaware limited liability company registered to do business in the State of Florida in the United States of America.

Jade Summer® is a brand owned by Fritzen Publishing LLC, represents the work of multiple artists, and is registered in the U.S. Patent and Trademark Office.

DELIVERY

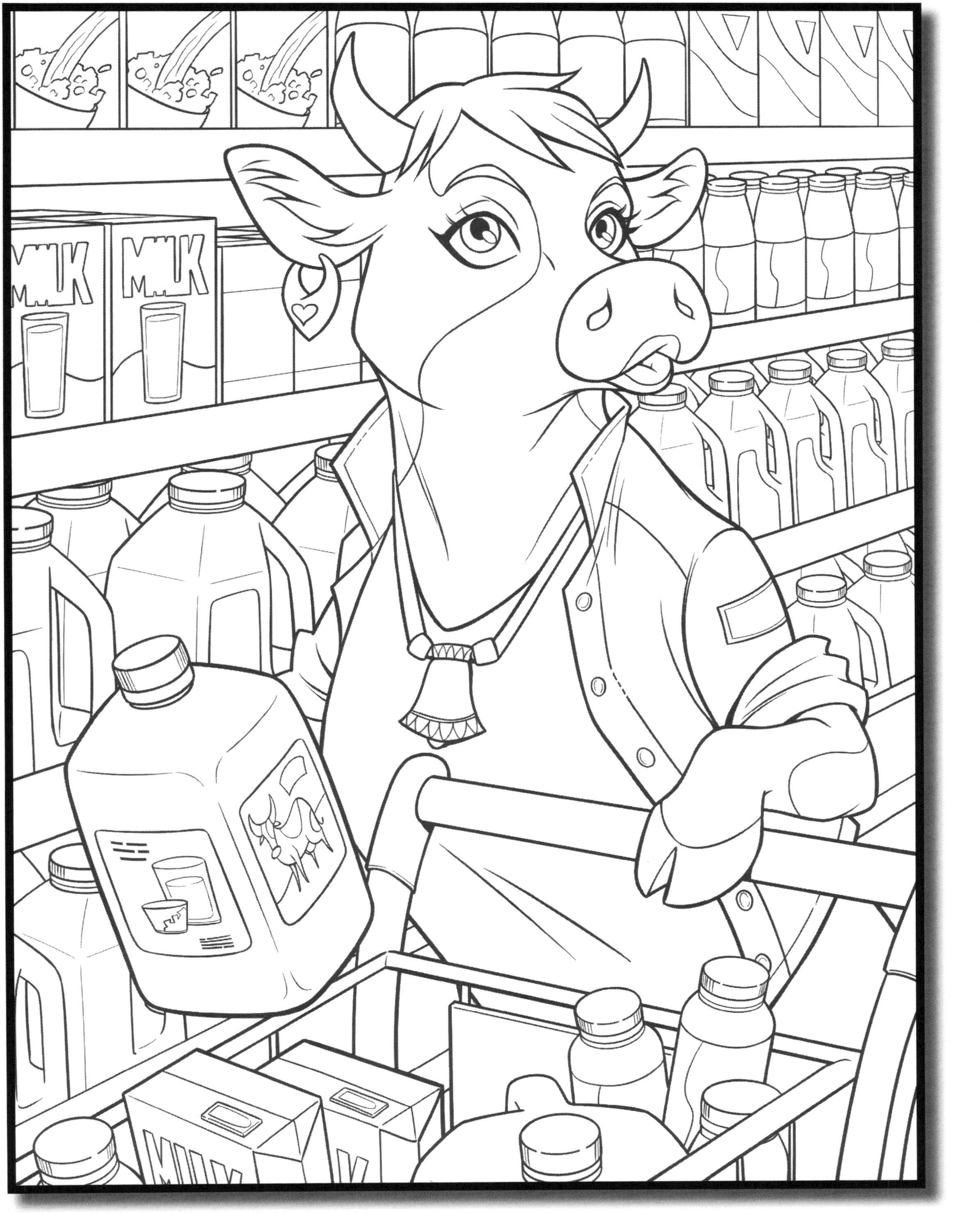
MILK

PONY

We have included a second copy of each image.

You can color your favorite images a second time, have an extra copy in case you make a mistake, or share one of our pages with a friend.

We hope this makes your coloring experience even better.

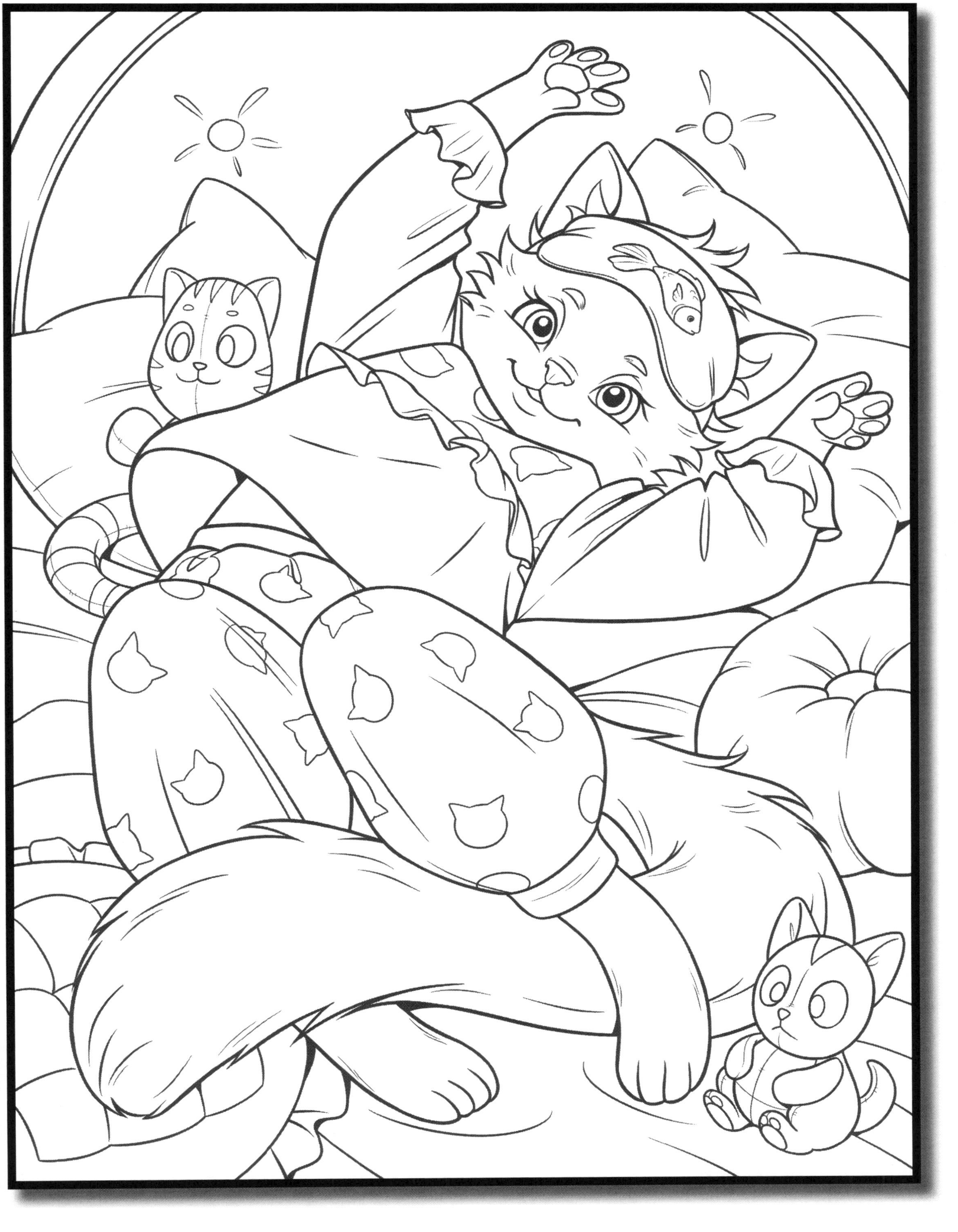

DELIVERY

MILK

PONY

P

NOTES

This page is for testing and documenting your color choices.

Made in the USA
Columbia, SC
07 April 2023

14766448R00061